David

The Giant
Slayer

Ethel Barrett

A Division of GL Publications
Ventura, CA U.S.A.

Other good reading in this series:

Elijah and Elisha by Ethel Barrett
Joshua by Ethel Barrett
Joseph by Ethel Barrett
Daniel by Ethel Barrett
Ruth by Ethel Barrett
Birth of the King by Alice Schrage
The King Who Lives Forever by Alice Schrage
Paul by Ethel Barrett
Peter by Ethel Barrett

The foreign language publishing of all Regal books is under the direction of GLINT. GLINT provides financial and technical help for the adaptation, translation and publishing of books for millions of people worldwide. For information regarding translation, contact: GLINT: P.O. Box 6688, Ventura, California 93006.

Scripture quotations in this publication are from *The Living Bible*, copyright © 1971 by Tyndale House Publishers, Wheaton, Illinois. Used by permission.

Published by Regal Books
A Division of GL Publications
Ventura, California 93006
Printed in U.S.A.

Library of Congress Cataloging in Publication Data

Barrett, Ethel.
    David.

    Summary: A fictionalized biography of the shepherd boy who killed the giant Goliath with his sling, made friends with the king's son Jonathan, and finally became King of Israel himself.
    1. David, King of Israel—Juvenile fiction.
    [1. David, King of Israel--Fiction] I. Title.
PZ7.B2749Dav   [Fic]   82-80009
ISBN 0-8307-0770-0   AACR2

Abraham	Joseph	Moses	Joshua	Ruth	Saul	David	Solomon	Elijah	Elisha
1900	1290			1000	925			722	

Exodus   Division of Kingdom

Contents

1. Can a Shepherd Boy Be a King? *7*
2. The King Is Asking for You! *16*
3. Adventures in a King's Palace *25*
4. Volunteer for Death? *30*
5. The Giant Killer *39*
6. Living with Kings Isn't Easy! *47*
7. Escape in the Night *58*
8. Treachery at Nob *69*
9. To Kill a King *79*
10. Stranger in a Foreign Land *90*
11. A King at Last—And a Promise Kept *101*
12. A Man After God's Own Heart *116*

Dictionary *125*

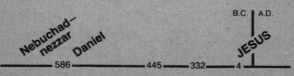

Ethel Barrett is one of North America's favorite writers and Bible storytellers. She is the author of over forty books, including seven in this popular Bible Biography series for kids. Her *Stories to Grow On* series was nominated for a Gold Medallion Award in 1979, and her recording of *Ethel Barrett Tells Favorite Bible Stories* was nominated for a Grammy Award in 1978. Ethel Barrett's books are available in bookstores everywhere.

Can a Shepherd Boy Be a King?

1 Samuel 16:4-13

There was a bear in the bushes.

It was on all fours, standing stock-still. David knew it was there before he saw it. First there was the rustle in the bushes. And then the twigs snapping.

Baaaaaa—

One of David's baby lambs, lying between two older sheep, lifted its head and then ducked down again. Then, one by one, the other sheep lifted their heads, startled awake from their afternoon naps.

David had been lying against a rock, partly dozing. Now he sat up straight, every bit of him tingling. He reached for his sling with one hand, and for his shepherd's bag with the other, fishing for one of the flat stones he always kept there.

His ear was trained to hear and identify every sound in those hills above Bethlehem. He knew every snap, crackle, and pop. And he could make a pretty good guess at the size of an animal by the sounds it made. This one was a big one.

David got up on one knee, slowly and carefully. He put a stone in his sling. And waited. All this without making a sound. Then the bear took a step and poked his nose out from the bushes and glared at David, its eyes blood-red and angry. David shifted his weight and got his balance. He pictured in his mind exactly what his timing would be, and exactly the spot he planned to hit. He pictured himself hitting it. He went through the motions in his mind. And then—

Pftttttttttttt!!!

He sent his stone whizzing through the air. It hit its target with perfect accuracy. The bear staggered forward, dazed. And then its forelegs buckled, leaving its hindquarters up in the air, before it toppled and rolled over on its side.

The sheep were all awake now, bleating and staggering to their feet in confusion.

David waited a long moment before he went

over to the bear. He stood over it to make sure it was dead, his heart pounding wildly with the excitement of the kill. Then he tucked his sling in his belt and went back and picked up his rod and his staff.

As he scampered over some rocks he called his sheep to follow him. He made a crooning sound to still their fears and calm them. Then he called each one by name and they scampered after him, anxious to get away from the danger. He waited for the stragglers, and reached down with his staff to help the weaker ones. "There you go, little fella," he said to a black one as he hooked his staff around its little woolly bottom and hiked it up over a rock. "And I'll bet you think you did it all by yourself," he chuckled.

David waited until the last straggler had caught up and then led them with long sure strides, following a spring-fed stream to better pasture. He was a good-looking lad, tall and strong, with reddish hair and beautiful eyes. His muscles bulged from the hard outdoor life he had led since he was a little boy.

He stopped for a moment and lifted his face to the sky. And thanked God that his beloved sheep were safe. And that the bear had been killed, and not himself. Then he opened his shepherd's bag and fished in it for his flute. The sheep were still jumpy and nervous, so he put the flute to his mouth and made weird and beautiful sounds with it to quiet them down. Then suddenly he stopped in his tracks.

Some men were coming toward him in the distance. Two—no, three of them. He shaded his eyes to see better. They were his brothers. But which ones? He had seven brothers, all older than himself. As they got closer he saw that they were his oldest brothers—Eliab, Abinadab and Shammah. David waited, legs apart to keep his footing on the hilly ground.

"What's up?" he shouted when they came within calling distance, but they did not answer. So he waited. And studied their faces. Trouble? He could not tell. Their faces were just *glum*.

"You're wanted down at the house," Eliab said.

"Is father alright?" David asked, looking from one to the other. "And our brothers?"

"They are alright," Abinadab said, and Shammah nodded his head yes.

"Then what—?" David began.

"Samuel the prophet is in town," Abinadab said, and he didn't sound too happy about it.

"Samuel?" David said, unbelieving. "*The* Samuel? The *prophet* Samuel?" He kept repeating it foolishly, trying to believe it.

"Yes," Eliab said impatiently. "*The* Samuel. The *prophet*. Abinadab and I will go back with you. Shammah will watch your sheep." And he turned on his heel to go. David put his flute back in his goatskin bag and hurried after them.

He decided not to say any more. He sensed that he was in trouble, but he could not imagine why. And he did not dare to ask. His brothers had a habit of calling him "brat." And if he wagged his tongue too much they called him "cocky brat."

He had learned long ago not to get fresh with his brothers unless he wanted to get his ears boxed. Or unless his father was around to protect him. And so he kept quiet, one step behind them as they walked back to Bethlehem. And so his head was in a whirl. He nearly bit his tongue off to keep from saying anything.

"Samuel did not announce that he was

coming," Eliab said finally, answering David's unspoken question. "He simply arrived, and announced to the town elders that God had sent him to Bethlehem to offer a sacrifice. He invited us to the feast."

"And when he told us why he had come, we were shocked," Abinadab began.

But Eliab interrupted. He wanted to announce this important news himself. "Yes, we were shocked," he said. "For he told us that God had sent him to *anoint* the next king of Israel."

David was so stunned his mind refused to work. Why had his father Jesse and his brothers been invited? Had Samuel come to anoint his father as king?

"Our father?" he began.

"No," Eliab said quickly. "One of his sons. One of *us*."

This time it wasn't only David's mind that wouldn't work. His body wouldn't either. He stumbled, thrust out his arm to catch himself and hit the heel of his hand sharply on a rock. He staggered back to his feet, stumbled a few steps, got his balance and caught up with them again. "And has he chosen?" he asked. "Has he chosen you, Eliab? You are the tallest—and the oldest—"

"No, he did not choose me," Eliab said. "Nor did he choose Abinadab. Nor Shammah. None of us."

"One of the others?"

"No. None of the others. Our father had each of us step forward and stand before him. And each time, Samuel said, 'No—the Lord says this is not the right one.' "

"But, Eliab—you are the tallest, the oldest—"

"Yes, yes, *yes,*" Eliab shot back. "But Samuel said the Lord told him not to judge by appearances. He, God, judges men by what is in their hearts."

"But then, what—"

"We don't *know* what," Eliab replied.

"That's right," Abinadab said. "After we all stood before him, he turned to father. And he asked father if there were more—"

Eliab interrupted again. "And father said, 'Yes. My youngest son. But he is a mere boy. He's watching the sheep.' And Samuel said, 'Send for him.' So father sent us up to get you. And here we are."

David thought about this for a moment. "Well,

then," he said at last, "he just wants all of us there before he announces his choice. Or *God's* choice. That's simple enough. We all have to be together. That's what *I* think."

"You're not supposed to think," Eliab said. "You're only a kid."

So David said no more. He was silent the rest of the way down to Bethlehem, through the crooked streets, and finally to the place where Samuel and the town elders were gathered.

Once there, David went to his father and kissed him, then stood there, silent. He saw his brothers standing about. And the great prophet. Samuel. Samuel with the white hair and great flowing beard, and eyes burning as if they were on fire. He bowed his head respectfully toward Samuel in greeting. He did not dare move.

And then—and then—

He saw Samuel reach into his girdle and pull out a vial of olive oil.

There was a great silence in the room—one you could almost *feel*. And then—

"The Lord has told me to come here," Samuel began. "And I have told your father Jesse that I would not eat the evening meal until I had obeyed

God and anointed the future king of Israel." He took the top off the vial of oil. And he walked toward—

David!

"In the name of the Lord," he said, "who has commanded me to do this—I anoint you, David, son of Jesse, the next king of Israel." And he lifted the vial. And he poured the oil over David's head. It trickled down David's neck and face, and onto his cloak.

David knelt before the great prophet in silence. He could not believe it. There was no way he could believe it.

Him?!??

The future king of Israel?!??

2

The King Is Asking for You!

1 Samuel 17:34,35

The weeks passed, and the months.
The hot summer months.
And then the winter rains.
And then it was spring again—
And David's life went on as it had before. He led his father's sheep across jagged rocks, cliffs and crags, rolling off into the desert. Up in the hilly country he looked for streams of water—always looking for water and pasture for his sheep.

So all was the same, and yet somehow different. For something had happened to David. He looked the same. And he acted the same. But somewhere way down inside him his love for God was growing and growing until sometimes he was ready to burst with it. It seemed to him that God was everywhere—inside him and all around him. He saw God in the stars by night and in the sun by day.[1]

He saw Him in the storms too, in the lightning. And he called the thunder the voice of God.[2]

When the late afternoon sun cast long shadows, David would start leading his flock toward the sheepfold his father shared with other shepherds. Actually it was just stone walls built in a huge square. It had no roof and no door, only an opening. At night the shepherds all led their flocks back into the same fold, and they took turns guarding that opening.

When it was David's turn he would roll up his cloak for a pillow and curl up in the doorway to keep out beasts and night prowlers. *He* was the door. He would count his own sheep as they went in to see that they were all safely home. He knew them all by name. Every shepherd knew his own sheep. And every sheep knew his own master's voice.

When it was David's turn he would lie there in the doorway and stare up into the sky. And wonder about that evening, so long ago now, when the prophet Samuel had anointed him king. How far away it seemed, and how unreal. It was like a dream, and he sometimes wondered if it had ever really happened. His brothers certainly acted as if it hadn't happened. They still treated him like a kid. And they still called him "brat."

But sometimes he caught his father Jesse looking at him strangely. Did his father wonder about it too? David did not know, for in their busy bustling family they seldom had time to be alone together and talk. There were the seven brothers. And two sisters. The big family was all together only at morning and evening meals—and David was out with the sheep, sometimes for long days at a time. But when he was home, at day's end they would wash themselves in the courtyard in huge basins their sisters had filled with water, and sit down to eat.

Sometimes his older brothers would go out on the town. And his father would gossip with his neighbors on their doorsteps. And David kept his thoughts to himself. It was lonely business, being a kid brother.

During the lonely times he would take his

small harp and play tunes on it that were so beautiful they seemed to come from another world. He made them up himself. And he made up words to go with the music. He may have been called the "brat" at home. But to all the neighboring country he was known as "Jesse's son David, the boy who plays the harp."

Baaaaa!

David was lying on the grass, daydreaming when he heard it. It was a terrified cry from the sheep. He leaped to his feet without making a sound. There was a young lion walking across a clearing toward the bushes. It was so sure of itself, it wasn't even hurrying, just sort of trudging along. And in its mouth dangled a baby lamb, mute and helpless.

David grabbed his rod and flew across the clearing. He leaped upon the lion's back as if it had been a small donkey. He grabbed it by its mane and jerked its head back. He raised his rod and—

WOP!

One well-aimed blow sent the lion sprawling,

its huge jaws sagging open. And the lamb rolled out on the ground—unhurt!

Phew!

David stood there a moment, breathing hard. Then he pulled himself away from the lion. And picked up the lamb. And carried it back to its mother. He was trembling with excitement and his knees were weak.

He had killed a lion—and there was no one around to tell about it!

Yes, it was lonely business, being a kid brother. But you couldn't say life was dull!

He was still thinking about it when he got back down home. He mentioned his fierce struggle with the lion at the evening meal. But that's all he did. Just mention it. For they all knew about such dangers. They had all taken their turn at watching sheep when they were younger. And they knew about greater dangers than sheepherding. For now that they were older, they were off hunting, and doing their stint in King Saul's army when their turns came.

David envied them, for they saw so much more of the country than he did. They hobnobbed with big, burly fighting men, and they knew all the gossip of the army and of the king's palace. Their talk was of politics and palace doings and army doings—and war. There was always the threat of war, for Israel's enemies were many, and the king's armies were ever watchful for an enemy invasion. It was never a question of would there possibly be an enemy attack; it was a question of which enemy would attack next. And how long the country would be at peace before more trouble exploded.

The talk at the table that night was not about David killing a lion but, as usual, about war and palace gossip.

"The country's going to the dogs," Eliab said, and the other brothers nodded, munching their food.

"Ah, son," Jesse said, raising his head from his plate, "you talk as if that were something new. I am an old man and have lived many years. And all I've heard all my life is, 'The country's going to the dogs, the country's going to the dogs.' We mustn't run the country down. I think it is a sin against the Lord."

"But it's true," Shammah said. "I know it's not right to speak against our government and our king. But King Saul has changed. He used to be wise and filled with the Spirit of God. And now—"

"How has he changed?" Jesse wanted to know. And they all began to talk at once.

"He's never twice the same. He keeps changing. When he is in one of his good moods he struts back and forth as if he owned the world. And when he's in a bad mood he sits and stares into space for hours. Even his officers and his closest aides hardly dare speak to him. He seems to be torn apart with the spirit of anger and suspicion. And jealousy. And temper tantrums! Sometimes he flies into a fury. And everybody scurries for cover to get out of his way. And suspicious? He thinks everybody's out to get him."

Jesse was staring at them now, in disapproval. "Come now," he said, "it can't be all that bad." But he knew better. He did not travel far the way his army-serving sons did, but he listened to the gossip with the other men when they talked on their doorsteps and in their courtyards at night. And it was true. The misery and the gloom of the palace had spread over the whole country.

Everyone felt it. It seemed to be in the very air. It did seem that everything at the palace was in shambles.

"But surely, King Saul must have responsible generals—" David began.

They all looked at him the way you would look at a sheep if it suddenly started to talk.

"Look who's talking!" Abinadab said scornfully. "The brat!"

"I only meant—" David began. But they all jumped on him at once.

"Stop acting like a king!" they all cried, for they were all thinking about the same thing—the night Samuel had anointed their kid brother with oil. They didn't like to talk about it. They didn't like to even think about it. If they didn't think about it, maybe it would go away.

"When Samuel anointed you, he probably meant that one day you'd be his disciple," one of them said.

"Yeah—or at the most an assistant or someone to take his place after he died—or something like that."

"But he certainly never meant that you would be a king!"

And they all laughed at such nonsense—all but Jesse. "Stop this talk at once," he said. "I will hear no more of it."

It was then that they heard the knocking at the outside gate.

It was a messenger. And not any ordinary messenger. But one from the palace—from King Saul!

And the message concerned David! Jesse's youngest son David, the lad who played the harp.

He was wanted at the palace—to play his harp for the king!

Notes
1. Psalm 19:1-8.
2. Psalm 29:3.

3

Adventures in a King's Palace

1 Samuel 16:17-23

David walked beside his donkey, following King Saul's messengers. He was too restless to ride. His father Jesse had sent a goat and an extra donkey loaded down with gifts for the king.

Breakfast had been both solemn and exciting, different from any breakfast they had ever had in Jesse's house before. When David started to polish off another load of barley cakes and honey, his brothers glowered at him. "Even on a day like this, you'll probably be the last one up from the table," they muttered.

"I'm a growing boy," he beamed back at them. He refused to be drawn into a squabble. Besides, since the prophet Samuel had anointed him with oil and prayed over him, he had a strange new love for his brothers. Just as he had a deeper love for God. It did not matter what his brothers said to him. And whenever the messengers were out of hearing, they said plenty.

"I suppose he thinks he's on his way to get crowned," they said to each other. And, "Maybe he thinks he's going to take Samuel's place as a prophet, or be King Saul's assistant." And, "King Saul's assistant!?! He couldn't be an assistant to one of Saul's donkeys!" And they all laughed heartily at their own jokes.

David chuckled now, as he trudged along, thinking about it. He couldn't possibly be angry with them. *I may be king someday, if Samuel said what I think he said. And then again, maybe I won't,* he thought. *But whichever way it goes I'm sure of one thing. I feel closer to God than I've ever felt before. . .*

The room they led David into was almost dark. He could hardly make out the objects in it. An important, bustling official hurried ahead of him and bowed low before a huge chair at the farther end. There was a man in it. He sat so still David did not see him at first. The man just sat staring straight ahead at nothing. Except for his eyes, which seemed to burn, his face was without expression. Was he King Saul? David had never seen the king close up before. Even sitting down, it was plain that he was tall. "King Saul," the official said in a nervous whisper. "We've brought the lad who is going to play for you."

Ahhh, so it was Saul. The king himself. David's heart beat faster. The nervous official turned to David. "Play," he whispered. The king did not turn his head. Not a feature on his face flickered. David got his harp into position. He heard the door close softly behind him. His head was hot and his throat was dry. For a moment he just wanted to run. *I might be able to play. And then again, I might not,* he thought. *I'm more afraid of this than I was of the lion.* But his fingers found the strings on his harp, and he drew from it the first haunting notes. And the music filled the room, every corner of it.

It splashed softly over everything, like liquid color, spilled and spreading. And it painted pictures. Pictures of flat stones skipping across a smooth brook. And water tumbling over rocks. Pictures of speckled shade dancing in the breeze.

And a still pool being surprised by a pebble and breaking into a million crinkles and laughing. And sheep feeding on a hillside. And miles of spreading green pastures. It was the peace of God.

The late afternoon sun streamed in through the high windows of the palace. And it caught the glory of David's red hair, like a flame.

A deep sigh came from the chair where the king was sitting. And for the first time he moved. He turned his head slowly and looked at David. David stopped playing, and yet his music seemed to still be there, filling the room.

"What is your name, lad?" The king said. David had been so lost in his music that he came to with a start at the sound of the voice.

"My name is David, sire," he said. The king stared at him a long moment.

"Who taught you to play like that?"

David looked back, unafraid now. "I am a shepherd, sire," he said. "I spend much time alone. I talk to God. And I put it into words to go with my music. I have many songs in my head. They all are my conversations with God."

The king had no answer for this. There was silence in the room. As he saw that the king was not going to answer, David played softly again. It was as if the two of them were all alone in the world. Then suddenly it seemed to David as if *he and God* were all alone in the world.

He looked up quickly when he heard another sigh.

The king was nodding. David played on long after Saul was asleep, at peace at last.

Although David did not know it that day, nothing was ever to be the same again.

4

Volunteer for Death?

1 Samuel 17:12-31

"Tell us, David," Jesse said, and he looked
intently at his youngest son. "Which way do you
think the war will go?" He looked worried, and
well he might be, for the Philistines had invaded
the land! Saul's army had gone out to the field to
meet them, and in that army were David's three
brothers—Eliab and Abinadab and Shammah.

David looked at his father and his other
brothers. They were all sitting in their courtyard
after the evening meal. They looked glum.

"I heard from the gossip," Jesse went on,
"that they are not actually fighting yet."

"I've heard the same," David said quickly,
trying to comfort his father. "They may settle it
by a contest." They all knew what he meant. Back

in those days many a battle was settled by a
contest between two warriors. One side would
send forth a challenger. And the other side would
send forth a warrior to accept the challenge. And
the two warriors would fight to the finish. The one
who won the fight, won it not only for himself,
but for his entire army. Thus the battle was
settled—but by losing only one warrior instead of
thousands. There was only one hitch. These two
warriors had to be volunteers. And until the
warriors volunteered, both armies pulled up into
their battle stations and glared at each other. Jesse
and his sons all understood this.

"Anyhow, King Saul has not sent for me,"
David went on. "So he must be out on the
battlefield."

They sat in silence, wondering, until bedtime.

David had divided his time between watching
his father's sheep and trips to the palace ever since
that first trip many months ago. He served in the
palace on a part-time basis. He was sort of "on
call." Whenever one of Saul's black moods
descended upon him, David was sent for. He
would leave his sheep with his brothers, grab his
harp, and off he'd go. His sweet music would fill

the air at the palace, soft and tender and haunting, until the king was quiet again.

The mood of the whole country was dark, as if a great cloud had settled over it.

"All the same," Jesse said at last, "I'm going to send you to the front with provisions for your brothers."

David nodded yes. He had left them so often to go to the palace they were all used to it now. They sat around the courtyard till long after dark, Jesse making plans for the next day. "A bushel of roasted grain," he said. "They'll need at least that much. And bread. Ten loaves ought to do it. And a cheese for their captain. A big one, one of our best. See that he gets it. And find out how your brothers are getting along. Come back and bring me word."

No one slept much that night. They were worried about the war in general and the three older brothers in particular. Long before dawn the next day the donkey was packed with the provisions and David was ready to leave. He said good-bye to his father and brothers and took off on the 15-mile trek from Bethlehem to the valley of Elah where the armies of Saul were camped.

Saul's army was camped up on one hill and the enemy army on the facing hill, with the valley between them.

David pressed his donkey on for he was anxious to get there before the heat of the day. Also a feeling of excitement was building up inside him, as if something was going to happen but he did not know what.

He found himself talking to God again, asking Him for strength—but he didn't know *why*. It was as if he had a task to do—but he didn't know *what*. Or someone ahead to strike terror to his heart—but he didn't know *who*. *Of course my brothers alone are terrifying enough to make me pray for strength and courage any day,* he thought to himself, chuckling. But it wasn't his brothers he feared, and he knew it. And it wasn't King Saul, for the king had become very fond of him, and he knew that. It was something else; he was sure of it. But what? He kept telling himself it was probably nothing. But the strange excitement kept growing within him.

When he arrived at the outskirts of camp the excitement all about him increased his own. For the Israelite army was even then leaving for the battlefield. He asked around for directions to the station where the baggage was kept.

He left his packages with the baggage officer and hurried through the ranks to find his brothers. He elbowed his way through the arrows and bows and slings and shields and spears.

He strained his eyes in all directions looking for a familiar face. There was no use asking anyone, for the men were shouting their battle cries, and the din was so great his voice would never be heard. So he ran along with the rest of them, stumbling more than running, until he got close to the edge of the hill that looked down into the valley of Elah. It was then that he saw his brother Eliab.

"Eliab!" he shouted. "Eliab!" And then he saw Abinadab and Shammah at the same time. All three of them were sticking together. They whirled around in disbelief, one after the other. "What are you doing around here?" they all demanded at once.

"I came to—" David began.

"What about the sheep you're supposed to be watching?" Eliab asked.

David ignored that. "Father sent me," he said,

"to bring you provisions and to find out how you are."

They just glared at him.

"The rumors back home are that it's going to be a contest. Is it?"

They ignored that as if nothing David had to say was of any importance. "Where did you leave our provisions?"

"With the baggage captain. Is it going to be a contest—"

And then he stopped. For the shouts and battle cries had stopped. Everyone was silent, waiting. And gawking in one direction. Over at the other hill.

A giant of a man was standing on top of it.

A giant! Why he was over nine feet tall! He had on a coat of mail that looked as if it weighed two hundred pounds! And bronze leggings. And a bronze helmet as big as a peck basket. And a javelin as big as a weaver's beam! And it was tipped with an iron spearhead that must have weighed twenty-five pounds if it weighed an ounce!

David's jaw dropped. And he just stood there, his eyes nearly bulging out of his head. He could not believe what he was seeing. Was *this* the challenger? Why any contest with this giant would be over before it began. Who would dare to fight him? To fight his armor-bearer would be more reasonable. His armor-bearer looked like a dwarf—what with the giant's huge shield he was carrying—and the giant himself behind him—

The giant interrupted David's thoughts. He raised his huge arm in the air and everyone got very, very quiet. "Do you need a whole army to settle this?" he bellowed. "Choose a champion for yourselves. And send him out here. We'll settle this with a single combat."

No one moved.

"If your champion is able to kill me—you win! But if I kill him—we win! I defy the armies of Israel!"

He waited for someone to challenge him. No one dared. Then he turned on his heel. And stalked back up to the top of the hill again, his armor-bearer retreating behind him, walking backwards.

David realized that he had been standing there with his mouth open and had started to drool. He wiped his chin with the back of his hand. "Who is he?" he cried to no one in particular.

Then several people began to answer at once. "His name is Goliath."

"He's from Gath."

"And the king has offered a reward for the one who kills him."

"And one of his daughters for a wife. How's that?"

"And he's been coming here for days, standing on the hill shouting insults. He insults the entire army of Israel."

And that did it. At last David found his tongue.

"Who is this heathen Philistine anyway, that he is allowed to defy the armies of the living God?" he cried.

His brother Eliab swung around at him in anger. "What are you doing here, anyway?" he demanded, forgetting that he had asked this before.

"I came because father sent me—" David began, "so what have I done wrong now?"

"You're a cocky brat!"

"I was only asking a question—"

"You're a cocky brat!" Eliab said again. "You just came to see the battle!"

David was too fired up now to quarrel with him. He turned to the other soldiers gathered around. "Who does this Philistine think he is that he can insult the living God?!?" he shouted. By this time he had gathered an audience. The soldiers were crowding around him. Who was this kid anyway, who was talking like a king? Was he serious? Was he saying that *he* would fight the giant? The word was shouted from one to another and it traveled like a brushfire until—

The word came back from King Saul's tent. Send the young man to him!

The soldiers getting the news, half pushed, half dragged David away. The last he saw of his brothers, their faces were agape in half astonishment and half anger. They seemed to be saying, *Now you've done it. You and your big mouth!*

And a few minutes later he was standing before King Saul!

5

The Giant Killer

1 Samuel 17:32-58

Saul stood there silent for a moment. And then—

"You, David? *You?* I inquired who the challenger was and nobody seemed to know."

"Yes, sire," David said respectfully. "I am the one who defied the giant."

"You are a mere lad," the king said.

David looked back at the king steadily. He knew now why that strange excitement had been gripping him since dawn. Why he could not sleep the night before. Why he had asked God for special courage. And why he had the feeling that something very important was going to happen. "Don't trouble yourself, O king, about the giant Goliath. I'll go out and fight him," he said.

"You are a mere lad," Saul said again.

"I am seventeen, sire."

"Seventeen!" Saul said. "Why Goliath has probably been in the army *since* he was seventeen—or even younger." And he shook his head. "Oh, David, David. Playing a harp is one thing. What you are offering to do is quite another. You are a boy. Don't try to play a man's game."

"I have fought with lions," David said.

"But you have never fought with a giant—"

"And I've taken my lambs right out of their mouths. I have killed both lions and bears. And I can kill Goliath—"

"But you are no match for—"

"I was no match for the lions and bears either. It was the Lord who saved me from their claws and their teeth."

Saul was silent for a moment, as if he were remembering when he was a youth. Then he signaled for an aide to help him off with his own armor and put it on David.

"Then go," he said, but he sighed as he said it. "And the Lord be with you."

David stood there in silence as the aide

buckled Saul's armor on him. The bronze helmet.
The coat of mail. The sword. He took a step or
two forward. And then stopped. The coat of mail
was too long. The sword dragged on the ground.
He looked like a little boy dressing up in his
father's clothes. "I cannot fight in these," he said,
unbuckling the sword. "I am not used to them.
And they are much too big for me. I'll have to
fight my own way."

Saul looked at him in disbelief. Did he intend
to fight with no armor? Was God really with him?
"Very well," he said aloud. "Go and fight *your*
way. And God be with you."

When David walked out of Saul's tent he was
escorted by the king's officers.

He hesitated for a moment, then turned aside
toward a small brook. He squatted down alongside
it. And very carefully and deliberately selected
five flat stones. He opened his shepherd's bag and
put them in. Then he straightened up. And armed
with only his staff and his sling, started for the
battlefield.

This time the soldiers stepped back and made a
path for him to go through. He did not look at
them. His eyes were straight ahead. He felt a

sense of great power over him and inside him. If he passed his brothers on the way, he did not know it. He saw no one.

It seemed to him that he and God, for those few moments, were the only ones there.

And then the giant Goliath appeared at the edge of the opposite hill. And started down toward the valley. There was a great silence as if everyone, to the last man, was holding his breath.

The giant strode forward, his steps slow and deliberate. He did not intend to hurry, but would slay this warrior at his leisure.

David never took his eyes off the giant. He got a tighter grip on his sling. And put a stone in it. It struck him all at once that Goliath's slow and deliberate steps were because his armor was so heavy and his size so great that he couldn't walk any faster. Why his great size was actually a handicap!

Then Goliath stopped in his tracks as he saw how young David was. Was this the warrior chosen to fight him, coming at him with a sling? And a stick? This apple-cheeked boy, this kid?

"Who am I?" he bellowed. "A dog—that you come at me with a stick?"

David never faltered. He was mentally going through what he was about to do, just as he had done when he killed the bear.

"By Dagon I'll have your hide!" Goliath's voice was an angry howl, like an animal.

David kept coming.

"Come here and I'll feed you to the birds!" the giant bellowed.

Not only the soldiers, but the very hills seemed to be listening.

"You come at me with a sword and a spear—" David shouted back, "but I come to you in the name of the Lord!"

Goliath took a deep breath, getting ready to bellow again, but David hadn't finished yet.

"This day will the Lord conquer you—"

Goliath was purple with rage. Had the lad taken leave of his senses? Did he want to commit suicide? How dare he—

"The battle is the Lord's!" David was shouting. "He will deliver you into our hands!" And he ran toward Goliath with the grace of a panther, loading his sling as he went. Then he stopped. And thrust his right leg backwards for balance. Swung his sling in a circle. Took aim,

and let it go—thrusting his body forward to follow
through—

PFFFFFFFFFFT—

The stone streaked through the air, sure and
true—and hit Goliath square between the eyes
with a—

THUNK!!

It sank into his forehead, the blood spurting
out and running down his face.[1]

Goliath looked astonished, and almost
comical, as he stood for a moment. His armor-
bearer took one look and stepped out of the way.
Goliath took a step forward. His big body
trembled and tottered on the second step, and then
he fell forward and hit the ground with a
THWACK.

The silence now was a different kind. In the
Philistine army it was one of total disbelief that
their champion had fallen. In the Israelite army it
was one of total disbelief that David had done it.
Both sides stared as David ran up to the giant. He
pulled the giant's own sword out of its sheath.
And, grabbing the handle with both hands he
raised it high over his head. And then—down it
came with a gigantic THWACK—cutting the

giant's head from his body! The force of the blow sent Goliath's helmet rolling!

Then David grasped Goliath's head by its long hair and held it up for all to see. The roar that went up now was deafening. And the Philistines began to run in confusion. And the Israelite army rushed forward, swooped down into the valley and up the other hill, after them. Soldiers and officers alike ran, shouting in triumph. David found himself standing in the middle of the valley, Goliath's head still in his hand. And then he turned and found himself facing none other than King Saul's great general—Abner.

And moments later, he faced King Saul himself again. This time, not as the apple-cheeked boy. But as the young warrior who had grown up in a few moments.

And standing next to King Saul was his son— Jonathan.

Jonathan! The famous prince! David had heard so many tales of derring-do about Jonathan. And here he was—in person!

Note
1. It hit him with the narrow cutting edge, like a Frisbee.

6

Living with Kings Isn't Easy!

1 Samuel 18:1-27; 19:1-7

David was used to Saul by now. But Jonathan—the heir to the throne! Why, his reputation as a warrior was as great as his father's. Or perhaps even greater. He had won one battle with the Philistines almost single-handed. Just himself and his armor-bearer.[1] And here he stood before David, smiling with admiration for what David had just done. And David thought, *He's older than I am, but not so very much. What a brother he would make! Better than my real brothers.*

"You will stay here at the palace with me," Saul interrupted his thoughts. "I have plans for you." And he turned on his heel to consult with Abner.

David and Jonathan stood facing each other. The look of love and admiration in Jonathan's eyes was something David had never known before. No one had ever given him any credit for anything. His brothers had put him down all his life. His father had shushed him. Except for God, all he could remember was being alone.

Now suddenly he felt as if he had come out of a tunnel and stepped into a great wide space. For here was somebody older than he, and far superior—looking *up* to him.

And then—and then—

Without a word Jonathan unfastened the cloak that was around his shoulders. And put it on David. And in this gesture he seemed to be saying, *You are the bravest of us all. No one else dared to fight Goliath. Including me.*

And he unbuckled his belt with the sword attached and handed them to David.

And then his bow.

And his eyes seemed to say, *You have behaved more like a king than any of us.*

David took them all in wonder. It would have been an insult to refuse them. He smiled in embarrassment. It just wasn't the time for words.

It was as if they could look into each other's heart. Neither of them had been loved in his own family. Suddenly now they had formed a little family of their own. They were "blood brothers." David felt that at long last he had a brother he could belong to. And he knew that Jonathan felt the same way.

All that was left now were the mopping-up operations before Saul was through defeating the Philistines.

A few days later they began the trek back to Saul's castle at Gibeah.

When the king returned with his victorious army, it was a festive occasion. A time to celebrate!

It was the custom for people to come pouring out of their homes and line the roads the king and his armies would march along. The people would sing and dance. (They were mostly women and children and older people. The fighting men were all off on the battlefield.)

"Saul has slain his thousands!" they sang. And Saul nodded proudly in acknowledgment. But then, as the songs grew in volume they also grew in words. "Saul has slain his thousands—and

David his *ten* thousands!"

What was this?

Saul—his thousands—

And David his TEN thousands!?!!

General Abner and Saul's other high-ranking officers darted quick looks at one another. And secret looks at Saul. And Jonathan shot worried looks—first at his father—and then at David.

And David?

He was looking straight ahead, still in a daze over what an exciting day it had been. He did not see the trouble ahead.

Within a few weeks the affairs of the palace got back to normal. But sure enough Saul fell to brooding again. And who better to soothe his troubled mind but David? So the king sent for David. And as he entered the king's chambers, it seemed as if time had gone backward. He entered the room softly and looked again at the great man, brooding in his chair. He thought of how frightened he was the first time he had entered into that room, an unknown shepherd boy. And now, here he was, the hero of the land.

As he drew the first haunting notes from his

harp, he thought of what a long way he had come since the hills of Bethlehem. He did not notice that Saul was watching him as a cat watches a mouse. He played on, and the notes began to shape a tune. He tipped his head upward and poured out his soul in thanks to God: "Praise the Lord, O heavens! Praise him from the skies! Praise him, all his angels, all the armies of heaven. Praise him, sun and moon and all you twinkling stars."[2]

He did not see Saul tightening his grip on his javelin. He played and sang on: "Praise him, skies above. Praise him, vapors high above the clouds. . . . And praise him down here on earth—"[3]

Suddenly a thrill of warning shot down David's spine. He looked up, all his senses alert, his muscles tensed. Saul was poised to throw a javelin! And it was aimed straight at David! And then—

Whizzzzz—

David sprang aside just in time. The javelin whizzed past him. And embedded itself in the wall. He stood there in shock, his face white. Saul was actually going to pin him to the wall!

Then everything happened at once. Aides came running from every direction. And David felt himself pulled almost forcibly out of the room. As they bustled him down the hall, he could hear Saul's voice: "Don't let him come back. I don't want to see his face again. And demote him to the rank of captain!"

Phew!

Well, things simmered down as they always did after one of Saul's outbursts, and David went about his duties. His friendship with Jonathan grew. And also his friendship with someone else.

Saul's youngest daughter. Michal.

David was in love!

He went around in a daze, bumping into palace furniture. And as Michal was Jonathan's kid sister, David found out soon enough that Michal was also in love with him.

Now it's hard to keep love a secret. It sorta snaps and crackles and sprinkles all over other people. It's been known to fill up whole rooms with quivers of joy.

So Saul sent word to David. "The king was delighted," his men told David. David should really consider becoming Saul's son-in-law.

Now David was in love, but he still had his head on straight. It was some kind of trap. Saul had something else in mind. So David was very cautious and he sent this message back to Saul: "How can a poor man like me find enough dowry to marry the daughter of a king? I am nothing. My family is nothing."

Now David knew well what he was saying. For a dowry was a bridal gift, usually a huge sum of money. And expensive presents for the entire family. Michal was a king's daughter; it would cost David a fortune!

Then David waited. And waited.

When the answer came back, David knew he was right. The Philistines were yapping at Saul from one of the borders. And the only dowry Saul required was evidence that 100 Philistines had been killed. "Vengeance on my enemies is the only thing I want," Saul said. *But I hope David dies trying,* is what he meant.

So those were the terms!

David knew Saul well by now. So this came as no shock.

"Tell King Saul I'll accept his offer," he said.

And it surely seemed that he had condemned himself to death when he said it.

And so the stage was set for what Saul hoped was David's execution.

David got his men ready and left for the border, and the enemy.

And Saul waited expectantly.

And Michal waited fearfully.

They did not have to wait long for the news to come back.

David had not killed 100 Philistines.

David had killed *200* Philistines.

He came back looking healthier than ever. And he was more popular than ever.

Michal was given to him as a wife. And they lived in their own house on the palace grounds.

David—married to a king's daughter! What golden days they were!

And it seemed that David could do no wrong!

And then, one day. . .

"David, I have to talk to you right away. In private." It was Jonathan. They walked a few steps up the corridor, alone together for a few minutes.

"I have to talk fast," Jonathan said softly.

"It's better if we're not seen talking together. My father wants you assassinated. He is talking about it to his officials. And to me. He wants you dead. That is his desire."

"He talked to you?"

"Yes. That was his mistake." Jonathan hurried on before David had a chance to answer. "Tomorrow morning, go to our hiding place in the fields. I'll persuade my father to take a walk with me out there where we can be alone. I'll talk to him about you. Then I'll get rid of him, and tell you everything he says."

And he walked on, leaving David standing there. There was no time to say any more.

David sat quietly waiting in the bushes. He saw them coming from the distance, just the two of them. And as they came closer, he saw that Jonathan was talking to his father earnestly. His father was nodding his head. He looked glum.

It seemed like forever; actually it was only a few minutes. Then Saul made his way back to the palace. Jonathan walked on slowly as if he were walking aimlessly. Then when he was satisfied that Saul was out of sight, he signaled for David to come out of hiding. David scrambled out of the brush.

"He was in one of his better moods," Jonathan began. "I reminded him that you had never harmed him. And of Goliath. And how you risked your life. I told him there was no reason for him to want you murdered. He just stared at the ground as if he didn't hear me at first. But he finally made a promise, David, that you would not be killed."

David looked at Jonathan, wary and cautious.

"There's nothing to fear," Jonathan insisted. "Everything will be just as it was before."

David sighed. Looked at Jonathan. And then grinned. "Alright," he said finally. "It doesn't matter what happens. God will be with me."

And they walked back together. The gloom suddenly lifted. It was like old times. Well, almost like old times. Things could never really be the same again.

Notes
1. First Samuel 14:1-23; or you can read the story in *Rules—Who Needs Them?* by Ethel Barrett.

2. Psalm 148:1-3.
3. Psalm 148:4,7.

7

Escape in the Night
1 Samuel 19:8-17; 20:1-42

The next few months went smoothly enough.
David was happy, and so in love with Michal!

There were a few skirmishes on the border
with their enemies. But David won quick victories
and was soon back home again. And Saul was as
friendly as a basket of chips.

David knew Saul's moods; he knew it could
not last forever. But he kept hoping. Right up until
the time when he realized it could not last another
day.

He was in Saul's quarters, playing his harp for
Saul, just for old time's sake—for Saul had been
in a good mood for many weeks now. The room
was filled not only with David's music but with a
sense of peace and good will. When suddenly—

Without any warning, Saul grabbed his spear and—hup!—hurled it at David! It sailed past David's head and embedded itself in the wall—quivering.

When the aides rushed in they found Saul, standing now, shaking with rage. And the spear still quivering in the wall. But David was gone. In the confusion, no one could tell where he went. And when Saul gave orders for his men to chase him and seize him, nobody tried too hard. David was able to sneak across the courtyard and back to his own house without any trouble.

The moment Michal saw him she knew something was wrong. David nodded yes to her unspoken question.

Michal put her arms around him. "Oh, my husband," she said, "and my poor, poor father. David, I fear for your life. You must get out of here before he kills you."

He held her close. "I'll leave in the morning."

She backed away and looked at him sternly. "No," she said. "You must leave tonight. If you don't you'll be dead in the morning."

He knew she was right. But he still argued. "I can't leave you here alone. When they find out

I'm gone—"

"They won't know you're gone," she said quickly. "I'll cover for you. I'll think of something. Now, quickly!"

She was already at the window, throwing the shutters open, looking down to see if anyone was about.

"Quickly!" she said again. "Before my father has the house surrounded."

He hoisted himself up onto the windowsill.

"Where will you go?" she asked.

"I'll go to the prophet Samuel. He's the only one I can trust," David said. He kissed her quickly, then disappeared into the shadows.

After he was gone, Michal closed the blinds. Then she got to work on a daring plan.

In the morning Saul's guards came for David.

"He's sick," Michal said. "He can't get out of bed."

They looked across the room at his bed. They saw him humped up in it, the covers drawn up over his head, a thatch of his hair sticking out.

They left then, and Michal waited, hardly daring to breathe.

In a few minutes they were back.

"We must take him to the king," they said, "even if we have to carry him *in* his bed."

They went over to his bed and yanked the covers off. But it was not David in there. It was a large statue made of wood! And the thatch of hair—was goat's hair! David was safe!

But it was many months before he saw either Michal or Jonathan again.

David had gone to Samuel's house in Ramah. And Samuel had taken him to Naioth, which was a sort of seminary for prophets. Saul had sent his men to pursue David. And when they failed, Saul went himself. He was bound he was going to capture David. But every time Saul got close to doing it, David seemed to slip out of his grasp the way an apple seed pops out from between your thumb and finger when you squeeze it. So finally Saul gave up and went back home.

Though Saul did not know it, David had come back home, too—but not to the palace. Instead he hid on the outskirts of the palace grounds, in a field. And sent for Jonathan.

They ran toward each other until they were a few yards apart. "Michal is safe!" Jonathan shouted. Then they stood still—and laughed. David laughed with joy. And Jonathan laughed with relief that David was safe. Then they got down to their problem.

Saul.

"I don't think he's planning to kill you," Jonathan said. "He always tells me everything. Even little things. He keeps nothing from me." David shook his head in disbelief.

"I know he'd tell me," Jonathan insisted.

"No," David said patiently as if he were trying to explain something to a child. "He knows about our friendship. And he knows you are loyal to me. If he were planning to kill me, do you think he'd tell you?"

Jonathan shook his head stubbornly. "I just can't believe this about my father."

"Jonathan!" David said in exasperation. "You're refusing to face it. I'm only one step away from death, and you know it!"

They were silent for a moment. They both knew David was right.

"Alright," Jonathan said at last. "Tell me what I can do."

"Well," David said, "tomorrow is the first day

of the yearly sacrifice feast."

They both knew what he meant. During that feast, everybody went back to where he lived if he possibly could. "Alright," David went on. "I'm supposed to come back to the palace. But I won't. I'll hide out in the field instead. If your father asks for me, tell him I've gone back to my own home in Bethlehem for a family reunion. And if he says 'fine,' I'll take it as a sign that I can come back. I want to see Michal. Maybe we *can* carry on as we were. I hope so."

"But if he's angry?"

"If he's angry," David said sadly, "I'll know he still wants to kill me."

They both agreed that was the way to go. There was one problem. How would David know?

"Easy," Jonathan said. "I'll come out near where you're hiding for some target practice. And bring a boy with me. I'll shoot three arrows as if I were shooting at a target, and the boy will run to get them. Now. If I shoot them in front of the stone pile, I'll shout to the boy, 'They're on this side.' That will mean all is well. But if I shoot them past the stone pile, I'll shout to the lad to go farther, that the arrows are still up ahead of him.

That will mean you have to run for your life. Have you got it straight?"

David nodded. "Yes. This side of the stone pile, all is well. Beyond the stone pile—I run."

"Right. It will be tomorrow, or the next day at the latest," Jonathan said. And then waited. There was something on his mind. "David," he said at last, "will you promise me something? When you get to be king—"

David held up his hand in protest, but Jonathan plunged on. "And you will be king, David. I knew it that day when you ran out to face Goliath. God is not with my father any longer. I've known it for a long time. God is with you."

David could not find an answer. Why, Jonathan was Saul's oldest son. It was hard to talk to him about things like this. David just stood there, his eyes filled with pain.

"As God blesses you, will you remember me? And if I have children—will you remember them?" Jonathan asked.

David swallowed hard. He could not speak, but he nodded yes.

"Swear it," Jonathan said. "Swear it by our friendship."

David found his voice. "I swear it to you, Jonathan—as my blood brother."

They backed away from each other then, and Jonathan became very businesslike. "Be at the hideout by the stone pile." And he turned and walked away.

It wasn't until the second day that David saw Jonathan coming back.

The first day of the sacrificial feast was uneventful. Saul was nippy, and everyone else was on edge. It was like the calm before a storm. But he did not ask about David. Everyone went to bed grateful that the day had passed without an explosion.

The second day passed the same way—until the evening meal. Then the moment came that Jonathan had been dreading. He'd been expecting it, waiting for it, and hoping it wouldn't come at all.

"Why isn't David here?" his father asked out of the blue. "He wasn't here yesterday. This is the second day of the feast."

Jonathan had his answer all prepared. But when he went to say it, his mouth was so dry he could hardly find enough spittle to swallow so he could get the words out.

"He asked if he could go home to his father's house in Bethlehem," he finally managed to answer. "His family wanted him to be there. So I told him to go ahead."

WOOOOOOOOOSH!!!

"You—&%*$*&$&%!!!!!" Saul shrieked at his son, and he called him a foul name. "Don't you think I know what you're up to? Don't you think I know you want this son-of-a-nobody to be king instead of you? You know as long as he's alive you'll never be king! I want him killllllled!"

Jonathan had been frightened before, but now he was angry. "What has he done" he cried, "that he should be killed? Why?"

He watched as Saul scrambled to his feet, knocking his seat over. Jonathan thought he was going to hit the table with his fist. But instead he grabbed his javelin that was standing against the wall behind him. He took a step forward to clear the wall. And then—whooosh! hurled it—straight—at—Jonathan. Straight—at—his—own—son!!!

Jonathan ducked instinctively before he had

time to realize what was happening. The javelin hit the wall, bounced, and fell to the floor with a clatter. Jonathan glared at his father in fierce anger. And he rose from the table and stalked out without a word. His own father!

The next morning, David watched from the bushes, looking for Jonathan. When he saw him and the boy servant in the distance he got back into the bushes and waited.

A few minutes later he heard Jonathan's voice—sharp, clear, louder than usual.

"Start running!"

Then, in a moment, the shout.

"Go on—go on! The arrow is still ahead of you! Beyond the stone pile! It's WAY ahead of you!"

David heard the boy running past the bushes. And past the stone pile. His heart sank.

Then Jonathan's voice again.

"Hurry—hurry! Don't wait!"

David had been up on one knee. Now he sank back, limp. He heard the boy walk back past the stone pile again. He heard Jonathan's voice in the distance, telling the boy to go back to the palace. He still waited, knowing Jonathan was waiting too for the boy to get out of sight. He finally stood and waited until Jonathan got there. He came out from the bushes then, and stood facing Jonathan. They clasped hands and wept unashamedly. For they knew they might never see each other again.

"Remember," Jonathan said at last, "we've entrusted ourselves to God forever."

David nodded. "And if we have children—" he began.

"*When* we have children," Jonathan corrected. "For you are not going to die, David. *When* we have children, remember our covenant with each other. If anything happens to me, you will be good to my children."

It was several minutes before they finally wiped their tears, and David turned away. "Good-bye, my brother," Jonathan called after him.

It was true. They were the only family each other had. David turned and watched Jonathan for a long time until he finally disappeared in the distance. Then he walked away, not knowing where he was going. He was an outcast now.

But he was in God's hand.

8

Treachery at Nob

1 Samuel 21:1-15; 22:1-23; 23:1-16

The next few events in David's life followed fast upon each other. And they could be summed up in one word.

Treachery!

First there was the incident at the town of Nob, where the priests of Israel lived. It was there that the worship of Israel was carried on. It was the chief priest of Nob whom David went to see. Ahimelech.

The walk there had been a hot and dusty one, and he was tired and thirsty. All the way there he tried to decide what to say to Ahimelech. He needed the priest's help, but if David told Ahimelech what had happened, and the good old priest helped him, and Saul found it out—

No—no. He could not do that. He would have to get help without letting Ahimelech know the truth. In that way the priest would be innocent. And Saul, knowing he did it in ignorance, would not punish him. So when David faced Ahimelech he had his story all ready. He spoke in low tones as if he had some top-secret information. "I must speak with you alone."

"Why is no one with you? Where are your men?" Ahimelech said, automatically lowering his voice too. "Is something wrong?"

"It's a private matter," David said. "I'm here on a secret mission. I've told my men where to meet me later."

"Ahhh." The old priest nodded solemnly.

"Meanwhile I must have something to eat. Something I can carry with me. Bread, if you have it. Five loaves would do. That would be easy to carry."

"There's the holy bread for the altar," the priest said. "We're just about to replace it for fresh. You can have the old bread."

"Good. How about weapons? I came away in haste. I brought none with me. A sword. A spear. Anything."

The old man thought a moment. "I have a sword," he said. "It's the sword of Goliath, the Philistine. It's here for safekeeping."

This brought David up with a jolt. "You have *that* sword here?"

"Yes. It's in a closet for safekeeping. You can take it if you want—"

"I'll take it," David said quickly. He wanted to get out of there without being noticed, for people from all over came to this place to worship.

Ahimelech got the sword and David buckled it on. It brought back a flood of memories. David had reached his full height now. The sword no longer dragged on the ground.

They busied themselves with the rest of the preparations. They paid little attention to a man standing off to the side, watching carefully. He was not just any onlooker. His name was Doeg (Doh-eg) and he was one of Saul's chief men—the overseer of Saul's herdsmen.

Meanwhile, David hurried on his way. No resting place was safe for long. He could trust no one to give him shelter.

So with the sword of Goliath, David headed

for, of all places—the city of Gath—the hometown of Goliath. He was hoping to stay there at least long enough to get his bearings so he could travel on.

But it was not to be. For the mumbles and grumbles among the king's officers began almost at once. "Isn't he the one people sing about? Saul has slain his thousands—and David his ten thousands? Isn't he that David? Well, isn't he?"

When David heard these questions he realized he was indeed in a hornet's nest. With no one to protect him, it seemed to him there was only one way out. It was a strange way, but he was desperate. Pretend to be insane! What else? There seemed to be no other way to go.

So he scratched on doors.

And drooled.

And let his spittle run down his beard.

Until—

"What is he?" King Asher of Gath bellowed—"A madman? Don't I have enough troubles? Get *rid* of him!"

So David fled in disgrace from Gath. But at least he got out with his life.

He headed for Adullam, back in the territory

of Judah. It was a Canaanite city. And this time he didn't fool around with kings and kings' officers. He hid in a cave.

It was here that God began to send him the small beginning of an army. Not an organized and equipped army. But an army ready for guerilla warfare. The men who came heard of David by word of mouth—the underground. They just kept coming—those who were in any kind of trouble. Those who were discontent with King Saul's rule. And those who were afraid of Saul. Until finally David found himself the head of at least 400 men.

It was then that he began to worry about his own family. It was only a question of time before Saul, in his anger at David, would wipe them out. So David sent secret messengers to Bethlehem to rescue them. He had his brothers sent to him. And made arrangements with the King of Moab to shelter his sisters and his parents, and give them his royal protection.

Then he settled himself and his followers in the forest of Hereth—right back in Judah. With all his wanderings he had not gone too far afield; he was still practically right under Saul's nose!

It was there in Hereth that he got the news of the greatest treachery of all.

This was the lowest Saul had ever sunk.

This was the pits.

It was about the town of Nob where David had first fled—the city of worship where the holy things of God were kept—*that* town!

The messenger got through David's security quickly. It was Abiathar, the son of the old priest Ahimelech! They brought him to David. He looked exhausted, and worn, and tragedy was written all over his face. David motioned for some of his men to get him food and water at once. "What happened?" he asked. "What's wrong? Is your father alright?"

"My father is dead," Abiathar said.

"Dead! Dead?"

"Yes. All the priests are killed. And their families. And their cattle. The whole town is wiped out. King Saul ordered it done."

"King Saul—"

"Because my father helped you."

David's face sagged in shock. "But they didn't know they were helping me! I never told them. I knew if I told them the truth they would have a terrible choice to make. They are innocent!"

"It was Doeg," Abiathar said. "He was there at the time. He saw you. He told Saul. And when Saul ordered us wiped out, Doeg was eager enough to recruit some men and carry out Saul's orders."

David put his head in his hands and moaned. "Oh, I should have known, I should have known," he said. "When I saw Doeg there I should have known. But I never dreamed anything like this would happen."

By this time David's men had brought food and water to the exhausted Abiathar. David sat down beside him as he ate.

"I've caused this," he said. "You must stay here and be under my protection. If anyone harms you, it will be over my dead body." And he put his head in his hands again and wept. If Saul could do such a treacherous thing to those innocent priests, what would he do to those who helped David knowingly?

Jonathan?

Or even Michal?

He knew now that for anyone who would help him, the cost would be very great. And he also knew now that it was going to be a long, long struggle.

It turned out he was right.

Saul's reign had become a foolish game of hide-and-seek.

As time went on, David's men became more and more skilled in guerilla warfare. And David became more skilled in strategy. And he had a direct connection with God! Abiathar became his prophet.

David had intelligence and counterintelligence just as we do today—spies sent out in all directions to let him know what was going on.

So when his spies told him that the Philistines were attacking a town called Keilah and robbing the threshing floors, he had other things besides Saul's treachery to think about. And he had direct guidance to God through Abiathar. "Lord," he asked, "shall I go and attack the Philistines and save Keilah?" The answer was yes.

But David's followers protested. They shuffled their feet and stared at the ground. "No," they begged. "We're frightened enough right here in Judah. We don't want to fight the whole Philistine army."

David went back to Abiathar to see if he had heard correctly. "Shall I go?" he asked again.

"Yes," the answer came back. "I already told you. Go to Keilah and I'll help your conquer the Philistines."

And that is exactly what David did.

It was surprisingly easy.

The Philistines were put to rout with no problem at all. And the people of Keilah were saved. And David and his men had a walled city to hole up in for a change!

A walled city!

A haven of safety! A place of comfort—

A death trap!

The thought hit David all at once and he stopped in his tracks. No sooner had he done this than his spies came and verified it. Saul had learned where they were and was already on his way!

"This is a ready-made death trap," David said. "Unless the men of Keilah protect me—"

But what if they would not!

"Ask the Lord if Saul's men are really coming," he told Abiathar.

The answer was yes.

"Then will the men of Keilah protect us?"

The answer was no. *They will betray you.*

By now David had about 600 men. "Saul is on his way here," he told them. "And God has told me that the men of Keilah will betray us."

David was neither surprised nor disillusioned. He knew what treachery was by now.

So when his men put it into words—"You mean the city will turn on us after we—"

"That's not the point," he said. "And there's no time to think about it now. Get ready to leave. Within the hour."

And so the chase went on. Zigzagging through the wilderness. Going around in circles. Running in and out of caves. Getting nowhere. What a pathetic waste of time!

It was down in the southern part of the wilderness in a place called Ziph where David had a most unlikely visitor—a person he thought he would never see again.

Jonathan.

9

To Kill a King
1 Samuel 23:17-29; 24:1-22

When David saw Jonathan coming from a distance, he leaped to his feet and ran toward him. The two friends together again at last! They held each other at arm's length for a minute, clasping each other's shoulders. Then they threw their heads up and laughed with joy. It was several minutes before they could sit down and talk sensibly.

"My father will never find you here," Jonathan said. "You have developed into an expert guerilla fighter."

"But so has Saul," David said. "It has become a contest of wits between us. I don't know where it's all going to end."

"End?" Jonathan cried. "You're going to be

the next king of Israel. God has willed it. That is what my father fears. This is why he wants you dead."

David looked at his friend a moment. "You're the only friend I have in the world, Jonathan," he said. "But I cannot ask you to stay with me. I would not want you to fight against your own father."

"Yes, I have to go," Jonathan said. "But I'll pray that God will keep you safe."

They embraced again and said good-bye. And renewed their vows to each other and to their children.

A few moments later Jonathan was gone.

"God keep you safe," David said under his breath. "Oh, Jonathan, God keep you safe."

So Jonathan was gone. But the relentless chase kept on.

"Saul's on his way here," David's men told him.

"So we move on again," David said wearily. And they did. Again. And again. And *again*. And Saul kept getting closer. All the while David was scrambling up and down hills. Hiding in caves. Until it seemed at last to David that God was

surely going to deliver him into Saul's hands.
Finally, it seemed that all Saul had to do was close
his fist and it would be the end of them all,
when—

A message to Saul from his home front!

The Philistines were raiding Israel on another
border!

Saul had to go back. It gave David and his
men a breathing space. But it was all too short.

David retreated into the wilderness of En-gedi,
a bleak region along the western edge of the Dead
Sea. There the limestone cliffs towered 600 feet
above the Dead Sea. And a huge stream plunged
from the top, leaping over the cliffs in waterfalls
down to the sea. And it looked for all the world
like a mountain goat. It gave the place the
nickname "Fountain of the kid." And the whole
area's pock-marked limestone outcroppings were
filled with caves.

It was there that David led his men. It was
there he decided to stay and hide. When they
holed in for a stay, all David's boyhood seemed to
wash over him again. For there were grassy spots
where sheep grazed. And wild goats climbed the
limestone rocks. And in front of nearly every cave

was a stone wall, built by the shepherds to protect their flocks from wild beasts and to shelter them from bad weather.

David went "house hunting" to find a safe place where his men could camp. He found a place called Wild Goats' Rocks.

It was there in a huge cave that the word came to David's spies. Saul had finished with the invading Philistines; he was after David again with specially trained troops—thousands of them!

David received the news with a nod of his head. Everything had to be said in low tones. For the cave was enormous. Every word echoed over and over again, back into the never-ending darkness; no one knew how far back some of these larger caves went.

David's spies told him that Saul was near— indeed making a cave-to-cave search in the very area around Wild Goats' Rocks!

David ordered the men way back into the cave, back into the darkness. To avoid a trap he stationed others outside, all throughout the area, both to warn him and to be ready in case Saul should attempt a surprise attack—there were many possibilities. David was talking them over softly with some of his key men. "Saul is crafty; the idea is to anticipate what Saul will do and be one step ahead of him when he does it." They were in the midst of this when suddenly their lookout came dashing toward them from the mouth of the cave, slipping in the limestone dust of the dry cave floor. He skidded the last few feet and squatted beside them.

"It's King Saul," he whispered.

David looked up quickly.

"He's alone," the lookout answered David's unspoken question. David raised his hand in a gesture of silence. And motioned for someone to go to the back of the cave and sound the warning for total silence.

Then they waited.

A long moment passed. It seemed an eternity. Every eye was fixed on the entrance to the cave. The blue-green moss that grew on the walls glowed with an eerie light. Then suddenly—

The silhouette of a man—

A very tall man—

David caught his breath.

Yes. It was King Saul. King Saul himself!

They were all thinking the same thing.

He had come in there for a rest stop!

They watched Saul grope his way in, remove his outer cloak, and lay it on the ground. Then he sat down.

David's men leaned close and whispered in his ear. "God said He would deliver him into your hands. Now is the time."

David shook his head no in the darkness. "He is God's chosen king," he whispered back.

Their whispers were so low that, as they echoed through the cave, they could have been the movements of a small animal or the whirr of a bat's wing.

"Go on, go on," the men urged. And David crawled forward, carefully, inch by inch. He could have slit Saul's throat, which is what the men expected him to do. He got closer.

And closer.

And pulled out a short knife from his belt.

And carefully, very carefully—

Took ahold of the bottom of Saul's cloak—

And sliced off a piece!

Then he backed away as carefully as he had gone forward. He managed to do it without disturbing a pebble. His heart was in his throat now. For any moment Saul's eyes would be used to the dark; he'd be able to see—and call for help!

Then the tense moment was over. Saul groped for his cloak, picked it up, and felt his way back out of the cave.

"Why didn't you kill him?" David's men whispered, louder now. "You only cut off a piece of his cloak!"

David answered quickly. "It's a sin to attack God's chosen—in *any* way."

That silenced their whispered clamoring. David was right. You just didn't kill a king God had chosen to rule over you.

They waited until they heard Saul scramble along the ledge and let himself down to level ground. They still waited a moment in silence. Then David scrambled to his feet. He put his knife back in his belt. Then started for the cave's entrance. Those who were close enough to see would have followed him, but he waved them back. Then he went out on the ledge. There he stood, legs spread, head up, waving the piece of Saul's cloak in the air.

"M'Lord the king!" he cried.

Saul stopped in his tracks.

And again, "M'Lord the king!" Louder this time.

Saul whirled around. And as he realized who it was, his jaw dropped open. For one brief moment they were both silent, sizing each other up. David looked at Saul standing there in shock—bags under his eyes, his face haggard and drawn. And he thought, *How he has changed. He looks like a tired, old man.*

And Saul looked at David standing on the ledge above him, taller now, and filled out, bronzed by the sun, his reddish hair in disarray—and muscles bulging in the glory and strength of his youth. And he thought, *How he has changed. He looks like a king.*

It was as if time stood still. And then the moment was gone.

"Why do you listen to people who say I am trying to harm you?" David asked. "Why, God delivered you right into my hands. Right there back in the cave!"

Back in the cave? *Back in the cave?*

No! David was there?

"Yes, I was there," David shouted as if he could read Saul's mind. "I could have killed you.

And some of my men wanted me to."

Some of Saul's men took a step forward. He put out his hand in a gesture to stop them.

"But I did not kill you," David went on. "I told my men it was a serious sin to attack God's chosen king."

And he held up the piece of cloth he had cut from Saul's cloak, and waved it over his head. "Do you see what I have in my hand?" he said. Saul could not answer. He just stared in disbelief.

"It's the hem of your cloak!" David cried. "I cut off the hem of your cloak. But I did not touch you. And I won't touch you. In spite of your wickedness, I won't touch you!"

Saul's knees were wobbly now. The ground seemed uncertain beneath him. It was only his pride that kept him standing up.

David continued to hold out the piece of cloth toward Saul. "Look at this! Doesn't this prove I am not trying to harm you?"

Saul swallowed, his Adam's apple bobbing, but he did not answer.

"Oh, my king," David went on, "stop and think who you are chasing. I'm as worthless as a dead dog—a flea—"

He watched as Saul's big frame began to sag. "Let the Lord judge which of us is right!"

Saul buckled and his face began to come apart, as if he had lost control of all the muscles.

And then he began to cry.

A few more of David's men had come out of the cave by now. They all stood there watching. The only sound was the waterfall in the distance, and the great King Saul crying. "Is it really you, David my son?" he sobbed. "You've repaid me good for evil this day. You had me in your hands. And you let me get away." He sighed. "I think some day you will be king," he said. "And if you are—when you are—swear to me that you will not kill my family."

"I promise," David said.

And that was it. David did not jump down from the ledge to meet Saul and embrace him. He just stood there on the ledge, silent and aloof.

After a moment, Saul turned to his officers and gave the orders for them to depart for home. And David turned and went back to his men. But not before he caught the look of hatred in the eyes of Saul's general, Abner.

"We rest up for awhile," he told his men.

"But we are not safe here."

"But the king's tears," they said. "Didn't he mean them?"

"Oh, he meant them," David said. "He meant them with all his heart—at the time. But in a few months, a few weeks, maybe even a few days—he'll change again."

And so the deadly game went on—

It was a question of who would make the next move.

And then some news came that made it look as if the game was going to be stalled for sure.

The great prophet Samuel was dead!

10

Stranger in a Foreign Land

**1 Samuel 25:1; 26:1—28:3; 31:1-7;
2 Samuel 1:1-12**

The prophet Samuel was dead!

The whole country was plunged into
mourning!

David's own personal mourning was great. For
aside from Jonathan, Samuel had been his greatest
source of strength. It was true, David had all of
his brothers with him now, and some of their older
sons. But none of them could be as close to him as
Samuel, or David's beloved Jonathan.

After the period of mourning was over, David
had to move on. He knew he wasn't safe there. He
knew Saul's changing moods. And he had seen the
look on Abner's face.

David moved his men to another part of the
wilderness, near the town of Ziph. And there he

set up his camp on Hachilah Hill.

It was not long before Saul came back with his specially trained troops and camped at the edge of the wilderness where David was hiding. The game was about to begin again. David made the first move.

He sent out his scouts to watch Saul's movements. Then when the time was right he took some of the men closest to him and started down the hill to where Saul's army was camped.

They crept down the hill, keeping to the shadows. There, before them on the flat land, Saul's huge army was sprawled, sleeping. In the midst of them was Saul, surrounded by his bodyguards. His spear was thrust into the dirt alongside him. It shone, a flash of silver in the moonlight.

They all looked like a gigantic painting; it was hard to believe they were real. It was also hard to believe that they were all sleeping. But they were. David waited a few moments to be sure. Not a soul moved.

"I'm going down," David whispered.

"I'll go with you." It was Abishai, the son of one of David's brothers.

David motioned him on and began to creep down the rest of the hill, Abishai following. Once or twice Abishai snapped some twigs and David shushed him. But there was no need to, for as they got closer they realized the soldiers were in such a deep sleep nothing could have awakened them. There was only one answer.

"The Lord must have done this," Abishai whispered. "He put them in your power."

David nodded.

Abishai straightened up, suddenly bold. "I could take his spear and no one would even know it."

David nodded again. They crept closer until they were standing over Saul himself!

"So let me do it. Let me put his spear through him. Pin him to the earth. He won't have a chance to make a sound. And I won't have to strike a second time. I'll kill him with the first thrust."

"No," David whispered, grabbing Abishai's arm. "He's God's chosen king. God will take care of him in His own time."

"And what if He doesn't?"

"Then he'll die of old age. But he's not going to die because I killed him." And as he said it he reached for Saul's spear and pulled it out of the dirt. Abishai sucked in his breath. "Get his jug of water," David whispered, "and let's get out of here."

They made their way toward the hill again, stepping over the sleeping men. They did not even try to be careful now, for they knew that *God* had put these men into this deep sleep.

When they were a safe distance away, David stopped, turned. He was grinning in the dark. When he could contain himself no longer, his voice split the silence of the night.

"Abner!" he shouted. "Abneeeerrrrr! Wake up, Abner!"

Abner struggled up on one elbow, then sprang to his feet. "Who is it?" he demanded.

David had a sudden desire to burst out laughing. "Why, Abner," he shouted, "what a great general you are! Is there anyone in all of Israel as great as you?" David could not make out Abner's face, but he imagined it, mouth hanging open. "Why hasn't the great general guarded his master the King?" he went on. "St-sts, Abner, this is bad business, bad business indeed. I swear by God, you ought to die for this!"

David waited; Abner had not moved. "So you don't think I was down there? Well then, where is the king's spear? And his jug of water? Look and see. You bet I've been down there!"

Saul was sitting up now. "Is that you, my son David?" he called out.

My son David, David thought. *Here we go again.* But he answered the king respectfully. "Yes, sire. I'm up here on the hillside."

Abner had whirled around and was staring at the spot where the sword had been.

"Why are you chasing me?" David went on, still respectful. "I've done nothing to you. What is my crime? You have driven me from my home. Must I go to a foreign land to be safe? You are the king. Why should you hunt for me as if I were— a—partridge?"

There was a silence, then Saul again. "Come back home, my son. I've been a fool! You saved my life! I'll not harm you!"

David waited until Saul had run down. Then, "I have your spear," he said. "Send one of your men for it." He said it without anger. He thrust the spear in the ground, and motioned Abishai back up the hill.

Saul's voice trailed after them. "Blessings on you—I've been a fool—blessings—"

David did not bother to answer; he'd heard all this before. Though he could not see Abner, he could feel his anger burning into his back.

When he got back up the hill, his men rejoiced. But David did not rejoice with them. He was very quiet. "Some day, Saul is going to get me," he said. "The only way I can get away from him is to go live with the Philistines."

And that is exactly what he did. And of all places, he went to live in Gath—and sought the protection of King Achish.

Once he had run for his life from King Achish. But now the king gave him a royal welcome, and even gave him a town in the suburbs to live in—a town named Ziklag. For King Achish knew that now David was a runaway.

What he did not know was that David was still loyal to Saul and to his own people.

The days and months stretched into more than a year. And David was secretly raiding idol-worshiping villages all over the countryside, stashing the loot away for the future. For he knew that someday he would be back in Israel—*as its king*.

It was during this time that his songs became filled with sadness and longing. "How long, O Lord?" he kept singing. "How long?"

Then suddenly it all came to a smashing climax, and in a way that David least expected.

King Achish decided to invade Israel and asked David to join him!

And what an army he had! Chariots! Horses! Equipment!

It was a vast and fierce army, not the kind David was used to. It did not matter, though, for David's position was the rear guard; the king wanted David and his men to go along with him and bring up the rear!

The army started its march northward. David's head was in a whirl. He was no longer his own master, head of a little band of men. He was part of something immense now, and matters were quite beyond his control. He was being asked to invade his own beloved country! What would he do?

He did not have to wait long to find out. He was out of command, but God was not.

The thing was resolved by King Achish's own

captains. For it dawned on them that when they invaded Israel, Saul's army would be in front of them.

They would be in the middle.

And that rascal David would be behind them!

They halted their march and confronted King Achish. "After all, David is still an Israelite," they cried. "What's to prevent them from squashing us between them in a giant pincer movement? You've got us placed in an impossible position!"

"But David's a runaway servant!" King Achish said. "He's been with us for over a year!"

"But he is still an Israelite!" they insisted. "It isn't safe!"

So the matter was taken completely out of David's hands.

"My captains insist that I send you back," the king told David. "They're afraid you might turn against them."

"Don't you trust me?" David asked.

"*I* do. But my commanders don't. So as soon as it is light tomorrow, pack up your duds and go back to Ziklag."

So the next morning, David and his little army

headed back to the only home they knew now.

They were about halfway there when they saw it. The red glow in the sky. It was in the direction of Ziklag!

As they got closer, their worst fears were realized. The Amalekites had raided their city. And burned it to the ground. And carried off all their women and children!

They looked at the smoldering ruins and wept. This was the most bitter defeat they had ever suffered. Their wives were gone. And their children!

David's heart had failed him many times with fear and discouragement. But this was one of the worst times. When he looked at the grief-stricken faces of his men, he had plenty to fear. For now, in their grief, even they might turn against him!

"Shall I go after the Amalekites?" he said to God. "Will I catch them?"

And the Lord said, *Yes. Go after them. You will get back everything they took from you.*

And David did. They all got back their wives and their children and all their possessions. Another victory won!

But what now? Their city, their homes, were

burned to the ground. Where would they go? What would they do? They were alone again—and in a foreign land!

Where, *when,* would it all end?

And then—

It seemed as if all the waiting and all the pain and all the wondering came to an end in one shocking climax. It came as a stunning blow. When David got the news he staggered backward at the force of it.

King Achish's army had marched deep into Israel, splitting the country in half. They had forced the Israelites to come out of the hills and fight against their chariots on flat land. It was a slaughter. The Israelites never had a chance.

And then what? *Then* what?!!?

King Saul was dead!

He had been wounded by an arrow.

And had fallen upon his own sword—

And killed himself!

And three of his sons had also been killed!

Only one son was still alive! Which one?

Which one???

Only Ishbosheth.

That meant Jonathan was dead.

David staggered back as if he had been struck.

Jonathan?

No matter what happens the rest of my life, David mourned, *I shall never forget you.*

Jonathan . . . dead.

11

A King at Last—And a Promise Kept

2 Samuel 5:3-12; 6:1-23; 9:1-13

Jerusalem!

The city that was like a great fortress. Built on the top of Mount Zion and shut away by deep valleys on three sides. Jerusalem—once the city of Amorites and Hittites. Now, Jerusalem—the city of David!

David strode back and forth on the roof of his palace, looking out over his city and into the valleys beyond. All the days of running and hiding were over. And the pain. And the grief. Yes, even the grief.

His memories of Jonathan were like a sweet song now.

David was home at last. He was king, just as God had promised.

He looked over the housetops and sighed. It had been a rocky road. For Abner had tried to get even for all the humiliation David had caused him. He had crowned Saul's son, Ishbosheth, king. And he had picked up the war where Saul left off. But in all the skirmishes, Ishbosheth's armies had grown weaker, and David had grown stronger.

To top this off, Ishbosheth and Abner finally had a falling out. And then Ishbosheth was assassinated by two of his own military men, leaving the northern part of the kingdom (Israel) without a king.

The field was clear for David.

In the months that followed, there was such a bizarre (unusual, strange, absolutely *unthinkable!*) turn of events, and they all happened so quickly, that David shook his head in a daze, even yet, thinking about them.

Abner came over to David's side!

The elders of the rest of the tribes of Israel came to Judah to make David their king!

A huge celebration!

Joy throughout the land!

Samuel's prophecy had at last come true! But now that they had a king—

They needed a capital where he could rule!

Jerusalem! Located right smack in the middle—between Israel and Judah—the perfect location to unite the whole kingdom!

And while the Amorites and Hittites were boasting that no one could take that city, David's troops s-n-e-a-k-e-d up through the *water tunnel* into the city. And the city was conquered.

And David moved in. And what a building program followed! David marveled at it now, as he strode back and forth on the roof of his palace and looked at all the buildings, and beyond them to the strong and tall city walls. He had built the city wider and taller than it had ever been before. King Hiram of Tyre had even helped. And the materials he sent! Cedar lumber! Carpenters! Masons! And all to build a palace for David!

The Philistines came back again and again to root David out, but he sent them back to their cities like whipped dogs with their tails between their legs. And slowly his enemies retreated and left him alone.

David was at long last at peace, and secure in his kingship—an undisputed *king*—and God was with him.

But one thing the city lacks, David thought. It was not enough that it was the great fortress city, and the capital of all Israel. He wanted it to be a HOLY city—a city of God. And, *One thing the city of God lacks—is the Ark of God.*

The Ark—that golden box with gold cherubs on top and a gold ring in each corner. It was carried by the Israelites everywhere they went in all their wanderings. The high priests and his sons covered it with badgers' skins and a blue cloth and put poles through the gold rings and carried it on their shoulders. Only the high priest was ever allowed to uncover it and look at it. Inside it had the Ten Commandments God had given to Moses. And a pot of manna—the food the Israelites had eaten in the wilderness. And the rod of Moses' brother Aaron.

The Ark stood for the presence of God. It had gone through the wilderness. Been carried across the River Jordan. Been kept in the Tabernacle in a town called Shiloh. Been captured by the Philistines—then rescued and carried back to the town of Gibeah and placed in the house of Abinadab. (Not David's brother Abinadab.)

David had no sooner thought about it when he

put his ideas into action. He issued the orders and
a plan was organized on a giant scale.
Representatives from every part of the country
came streaming in from every direction. And off
they went, to Gibeah, to the house of Abinadab.
The Ark had been there for nearly thirty years.

But here is where David went amiss.

They lifted the Ark out of its place and put it
on a *brand new cart* that was pulled by oxen. No
Levite priests. No poles in golden rings.

Hup—up on the cart the Ark went. And
Abinadab's sons—Uzzah and Ahio took charge.
Uzzah drove the oxen. And Ahio walked in front,
followed by David and other leaders of Israel.

Gibeah. It was hilly country and it was hard
going, the oxen struggling to keep their footing,
the cart swaying from side to side. But what a
joyous procession it was! They waved branches of
juniper trees. They played lyres and harps and
tambourines and cymbals—

It was a procession of joy, right up until—

Halt! Whoa! Hold itttttttt!—

The procession stopped with skids and grunts
and huffs and puffs and heavy breathing.

Something had happened. Something bad.

David sprinted back, panic-stricken. Everyone scattered, getting out of his way. He was afraid to even think of what he might find. Had the Ark tumbled off the cart? He did not even dare think of it. He got back to the cart, breathing hard. Uzzah was sprawled on the ground—dead.

David stared in disbelief. "What happened?" he asked.

"The cart tipped," they all said at once. "He reached out to steady it. He touched it. He touched the Ark of God."

David's shock and horror all came tumbling out in sudden anger. Why had God done this? He, David, was only trying to bring the Ark back to Jerusalem. Why? *Why?*

And then the anger turned to fear. What had he done? He had put the holy Ark of God on a *cart*. Why the heathen idol-worshipers carried their idols on carts! He stared into space for a moment. Everyone waited.

Then finally, "Make a stretcher for Uzzah," David said. "We'll march on. We'll leave the Ark at the house of Obed-edom (a Levite priest)."

And so they left the Ark there and went home in silence. David realized that he had made one of

the most colossal blunders (a *big* blunder; he had
really goofed!) of his life. It was months before he
got over it. For he had run roughshod over God's
holy rules. Now, for the first time in his life,
David was afraid of God.

He grieved over this thing for months. But he
was afraid to do anything about it. And there was
no word from God. Just silence.

Then, after a few months, the whole sorry
business cleared up like a bright morning after a
storm. For good news came back from Obed-
edom the priest. God was blessing Obed-edom and
his household and everything he touched!

Hallelujah!

This was it!

God was not angry!

The Ark could come home!

This time David vowed he would do it right.
The Ark was to be carried only by Levite priests.
On poles.

It was never to be touched.

It was not to be taken lightly.

It was the holiest of all the holy things of God.

This time the march back into Jerusalem was
not one of silent grief and shame. It was with the

crash of cymbals and the clickity-click of castanets, and the sweet strains of harps and lyres and the zinging of tambourines—

And oh, the singing! It seemed to split the skies! And the dancing!

And David was the "danciest" of all! He was leaping into the air for sheer joy!

The people gathered at the gates as the procession entered. And lined the streets in the city—laughing, cheering and leaping for joy.

The Ark was coming! The Ark was coming! Covered with a veil. And the badger skins. And the blue cloth. With the poles in the golden rings carried on the shoulders of Levite priests. The glory of God Himself was coming into Jerusalem!

It ws the *holy* city at last!

Jerusalem!

The Ark was carried to the place David had prepared for it—a tent like the Tabernacle in the wilderness. It was carried carefully inside. And that tent became a holy-of-holies, for it sheltered the Ark of the holy God.

What a day! What a celebration! David ordered gifts for everyone. Bread! Wine! A cake of raisins!

Then David dashed into the palace to greet his family and to find Michal. He knew she had watched from a window. How happy she would be! He could hardly wait to tell her all about it so she could rejoice with him.

He rushed into their chambers. And took one look at her face. And stopped short.

He was wearing an ephod—not the elaborate ankle-length ephod—but the simple linen ephod of an ordinary priest. It barely covered him. It was little more than a loincloth. Michal was staring at it in disgust.

"The king!" she said. "The king of Israel! How glorious the king looked today! In *that*!" She spat the words out, pointing to this ephod.

"Dancing in the streets—in public—exposing himself to the girls along the streets, like a common—like a common—" She was so angry she could hardly finish.

"I was dancing before the Lord—"

"In a *common linen ephod?* You might as well have been dancing in your underwear!"

"—before the Lord, who chose me above your father—"

"You looked like a fool!"

"—the Lord who appointed me leader of Israel—"

"You looked like a fool!"

"So I looked like a fool! I'm willing to act like a fool in order to show my joy in the Lord—"

"Like a fool!"

"I'm willing to look even more like a fool!"

She did not answer this time. Just stared at him. And suddenly, her real feelings were clear. What she was thinking showed in her face. She was a *king's* daughter. And he was a shepherd—an *upstart*.

David was suddenly spent, silent. All the ginger had gone out of him. He could think of nothing more to say. For in her eyes, in her face, he knew the truth.

She *despised* him.

It was a moment before he could gather the strength to turn and walk out. *I'd better get my love out of here,* he thought, *before it dies of the cold.*

He was always kind to her after that, always respectful and polite. But he never took her in his arms again, never touched her. And she never had any children.

Peace was at last upon the land. There were skirmishes with the surrounding idol-worshiping countries, but David came away from all of them triumphant. He was famous all over the land. He ruled with justice and fairness and everyone loved him. Everyone knew that God was with him.

It was the custom for a new king to have all the sons of the previous king killed so they could not rise up and claim the throne. It did seem like a harsh thing to do, but everyone accepted it. So no one was surprised when David asked the question. He was with his advisers and they were going over the business of the day.

"Is Jonathan's family all gone?" he asked. "Is there anyone left?"

It came out of the blue, and David's advisers knew what he meant. He meant, did Jonathan have any sons? One of the advisers spoke up. "The only one who would know would be Ziba— he had been Saul's chief steward."

"Send for him," David said quietly.

When Ziba was brought in to face King David he looked a little frightened, as if he were finally facing something he had been dreading for a long time.

"Yes, sire," he said. "There is one son left. His name is Mephibosheth. He's a young man now. And he is hiding—er—living—I mean he's *living*—in Lo-debar. At the home of a man named Machir. But he would cause you no trouble, sire. He is lame."

David turned to his officers. "Bring him here to me. As soon as possible."

His orders were carried out, and a few days later he was told that Mephibosheth was at the palace and would be brought to him in his quarters.

As David waited, memories flooded over him. He remembered himself, a mere shepherd boy, being ushered in before the great King Saul. And how he had stood before the moody king in fear and trembling. And now *he* was the king, and Saul's own grandson was about to be ushered in to face him. Would he too come in fear and trembling?

Mephibosheth was brought in before David could answer his own question. And yes, he was obviously frightened half out of his wits. He walked with great difficulty, supported by a servant. And he bowed low, and he kept his head down, looking at the floor.

"Lift your head," David said softly. "Look at me." The young man looked at David briefly, then lowered his eyes. It was plain to see that he expected a death sentence.

"You are Mephibosheth, Jonathan's son?"

"Yes, sire."

David gestured toward the crippled feet.

"Do you want to tell me about it?" he asked. "How did it happen?"

"It happened the day my father was killed, sire. I was five years old."

"You remember it?"

"Oh yes. I was old enough to understand. I knew my father and grandfather were at war. I was in the palace with my nurse. I knew by the whispering and by the way my nurse was acting that things were going badly.

Then I heard them whisper that my father was dead. I couldn't understand it. My father was the bravest man in all the world. How could he be dead?"

"Your father *was* the bravest man in the world," David said softly. "Go on."

"Well, my nurse swooped me up in her arms

and started running after some guards. I didn't know what was going on. I just knew they were taking me someplace. But then she stumbled. And she dropped me. Then I remember a long ride in the dark. They took me to Lo-debar, to Machir's house. When they stood me on my feet, I screamed with pain. I didn't understand any of it then. It was a long time before I realized that I was a cripple. And that I was no longer a prince's son. And that I was as good as dead. But the greatest pain of all was that my father was gone."

"Your grandfather?" David asked.

"He was cold and distant. I scarcely remember him at all. But I loved my father."

There was a silence. And then, "I loved your father, too," David said. "And we promised each other we would be friends forever. And that we would watch out for each other's children. I want to keep that promise now."

Mephibosheth fell to the ground. "Who am I," he said, "that the king should show kindness to a dead dog like me?"

"Get up," David said kindly.

Mephibosheth struggled to his feet with great difficulty and stood, leaning upon the servant.

David signaled for Ziba to be brought in.

"I have given Mephibosheth all of King Saul's property. I put you in charge. You will farm his land—you and your sons and your servants. But he will live here in the palace with me. He will be like one of my own sons."

David looked at his "new son" and smiled. And for a moment he did not look like a king at all, but like a father. And Mephibosheth looked back, his face flooded with relief and gratitude and love.

"You need never be afraid again," David said. "My word to you is as good as it was to your father. And he was the closest friend I ever had."

He stood there and embraced Mephibosheth. And for a moment, just for a moment, it seemed as if Jonathan was in the room. . .

12

A Man After God's Own Heart

2 Samuel 11:1—12:13; 14:25-15:12;
18:6-33; 1 Kings 1:5-37; Luke 2:1-14

Golden days!

David had built up the most powerful empire
in the world. Everything God promised had come
to pass!

He enjoyed all the rights and privileges of a
great king. He governed his conquered territories
through his own appointed officials, as he had a
right to. He opened highways and trade routes and
built whatever he wanted, as he had a right to. He
took for his own a woman who was already the
wife of another man, as he had a right—

Wait a minute.

Wait a minute.

He had a *right* to? Not as a king whose whole
life had been ordered by God did he have a right

to. No. Never. *Never.*

The woman's name was Bathsheba. And right or not, David took her while her husband Uriah was away at war. And as if that were not bad enough, David sent Uriah to the most dangerous spot in the battle—where he was killed!

But surely David, who had hardly done a wrong thing in his life, could get away with this. Surely God would overlook it.

The Bible gives us the answer in one short sentence. *But the Lord was very displeased with what David had done.*

Very.

But did God tell David this in so many words? No. He sent the prophet Nathan to speak to David in such a way that David could figure it out for himself.

"I want to tell you a story," Nathan said. And David settled down to listen, all interest.

"In a certain city lived two men," Nathan began. "One was very rich. He owned thousands of goats and sheep and cattle. And the other was very poor. He owned nothing—except one little lamb. And oh, how he loved that little lamb. He fed it from his own plate; he let it drink from his own cup. And he cuddled it in his arms. And then, one day—"

David leaned forward. He loved stories. He could almost fancy putting this one to music as he listened.

"One day," Nathan said, "the rich man had guests. And he wanted to feed them. Now the right thing for him to do would be to take a lamb from his own flocks to serve his guests. But instead—"

David was all attention. "Instead, what?" he wanted to know.

"Instead," Nathan said, "he took the *poor man's* lamb, and had it killed to serve his guests."

David's mouth dropped open. "I swear by the living God," he cried, "any man who would do a thing like that should be put to death. Have him restore four lambs for the one he stole!" David knew by now that Nathan was telling him about a real case, and asking him for his judgment in the matter. "He must be punished—!"

"The man is you," Nathan said quietly.

David stopped short, staring at Nathan.

"Yes," Nathan said. "You are the man. You took Bathsheba, who was Uriah's love and his wife. And God has told me to tell you this: 'I made you King of Israel, David. I saved you from Saul's power. I gave you a great kingdom. And if that had not been enough I would have given you much much more. Why have you despised my laws? Why have you done this terrible thing?' "

David slumped in his chair and put his head in his hands. "It is against you, Lord, that I have sinned and done this terrible thing," he moaned.

He sat there long after Nathan had left, and far into the night. It was then that he penned one of the most beautiful Psalms in the Bible (Psalm 51). He was sorry. And God forgave him.

But the golden years were ended. From here on out it seemed that David's life was all down hill.

First it was his son Absalom. Absalom— famous for his good looks, his beautiful long hair—and his *charm*. Wherever he went, people gathered around to be near him. But alas—he was also a smart aleck.

For David had spoiled him.

All his life, anything Absalom wanted, Absalom got. And when he disobeyed he was never corrected. So when he grew into young manhood—he was still a spoiled brat! Until the day came when he thought he was more important than his own father. And all the years of "spoiling" blew up in David's face.

For Absalom gathered some followers. And organized a rebellion against his father. And set about to declare himself king!

It was a staggering blow, worse than anything David got from King Saul.

Absalom!

The war that followed was dreadful. It was filled with sneaky plots and intrigue beyond belief. (There is not room here to tell the whole story; you can read about it in 2 Sam., chapters 15-18.)

But that last battle! What a tragedy!

When Absalom realized his army was defeated, he jerked his mule around and it ran pell-mell through the forest, absolutely terrified. Then suddenly Absalom was yanked back with such force he thought his neck had been broken. His mule was no longer beneath him. It had run ahead, leaving him hanging from a tree—his beautiful long hair caught in a branch! And while he swung there helplessly, some of David's men caught up with him. And killed him.

Back in the city, David was sitting at the gate, waiting for news of the battle. When the messengers came, he did not ask how the battle was going. "What of Absalom?" he asked. "Is he safe?"

No, the answer came back, Absalom was dead.

David turned on his heel and climbed up the stairs to the top of the city wall, weeping, "Oh my son Absalom, my son, my son—if only I could have died for you, oh Absalom, my son, my son. . ."

David had spoiled his son. And he paid a high price for it. His heart was broken. But there was more to come. . .

After Absalom, there was Adonijah. And alas, David had spoiled this son too! And in time, Adonijah also got too big for his toga.

David was a very old man now. He was confined to his bed most of the time. Why not, Adonijah reasoned, crown *himself* king? (Of course he had overlooked one thing—his kid brother, Solomon!)

So he gathered some followers (here we go

again!). He did not start a war. Instead, he went outside Jerusalem, and there he arranged a feast for his own coronation!

But another drama was unfolding back in the palace. The prophet Nathan—remember him?—sneaked off to the women's quarters and told Bathsheba about it. "Do you realize that Adonijah is staging his own coronation? That he has declared himself to be the next king?"

"Adonijah!" Bathsheba turned pale. Why David had sworn by God that *Solomon* was to be the next king!

Now the plot thickened, and quickly. No time to lose! Nathan and Bathsheba hurried off to David in his quarters.

Bathsheba went in first to set the stage.

"My Lord," she said, "you vowed to me by God that our son Solomon would sit on your throne. And Adonijah is proclaiming himself to be the new king."

Before David could gather his wits, Nathan came in. "My Lord," he said, "has this been done with your knowledge? Have you appointed Adonijah to be the next king? He is, even now, staging his own coronation!"

David turned to Bathsheba. And issued a decree to announce what had been promised many years before. "I decree that our son Solomon will sit upon my throne, just as I swore by God to you before. Call Zadok the priest. And the head of my bodyguards."

Moments later, David's officials and Nathan gathered around David's bed and waited for him to speak. He strained forward on his pillows, holding himself up on his elbows. His hair was white now, and his face was pale. But his eyes were bright and glowing, and for a moment—just for a moment—the grand old man seemed strangely young again. All the old fire was there, and the passion and the hopes and dreams were there. He seemed like the ruddy-faced boy who had played his harp for Saul so many years before.

For one brief moment he was absolutely in command again. He gave his instructions. And though his voice trembled, his orders were crisp, and they had the zing and the air of authority about them that had always overwhelmed the people all during his reign.

Everyone snapped to attention and scattered to do his bidding.

Adonijah's "coronation" was nipped in the bud. AND SOLOMON WAS DECLARED THE NEXT KING OF ISRAEL.

But David's time was up.

His days were nearly over.

But his NAME was to go on forever. For the last words he spoke were, "It is MY FAMILY [God] has chosen!. . ." (2 Sam. 23:5).

And he was so right! For it was from David's family that, hundreds and hundreds of years later, the LORD JESUS CHRIST was born!

And David? He went down in history as a "man after God's own heart."

Dictionary

Ark of the Covenant. A special chest or box God told Moses to build. It was a symbol of God's presence with the Israelites. The box was constructed of acacia wood and covered with gold, inside and out. At first it held the Ten Commandment tablets and later a bowl of manna and Aaron's rod were added.

Armor-bearer. A person who carried the large shield and necessary weapons for a king or army officer.

Prophet or prophetess. A man or woman to whom God gave His messages for different persons or groups of people. A spokesperson.

Psalm. A Hebrew song or poem usually praising God or expressing the deep feelings of God's people.

Tabernacle. The movable temple of the Israelites. It contained two rooms: the Holy Place, or sanctuary, and the Holy of Holies which contained the Ark of the Covenant.

Temple. The one central place in Israel to worship God. The first Temple was built by Solomon following instructions given by God to Solomon's father, David.

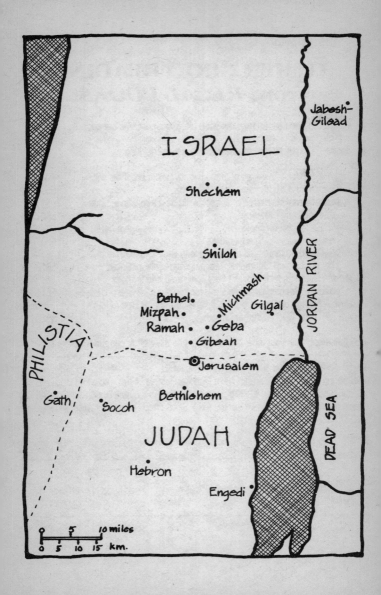